CHILDREN IN HISTORY

Vikings

Kate Jackson Bedford

SEA-TO-SEA
Mankato Collingwood London

This edition first published in 2011 by
Sea-to-Sea Publications
Distributed by Black Rabbit Books
P.O. Box 3263, Mankato, Minnesota 56002

Printed in China, Dongguan

Library of Congress Cataloging-in-Publication Data

Bedford, Kate.
   Vikings / Kate Jackson Bedford.
        p. cm. -- (Children in history)
   Includes index.
   ISBN 978-1-59771-272-9 (lib. bdg.)
  1. Vikings--Juvenile literature. 2. Vikings--Social life and
customs--Juvenile literature. I. Title.
   DL66.B43 2011
   948'.022--dc22

                                        2009044875

9 8 7 6 5 4 3 2

Published by arrangement with the Watts Publishing
Group Ltd, London.

Series editor: Jeremy Smith
Art director: Jonathan Hair
Design: Jane Hawkins
Cover design: Jane Hawkins
Picture research: Diana Morris

Picture credits: Ashmolean Museum Oxford /Bridgeman Art
Library: front cover tc. Luciana Bueno/Shutterstock: 28b. DK
Images: 29. Mary Evans Picture Library: 12cr, 20bl, 24tr, 26tr.
Mary Evans Picture Library/Alamy: 18tr. Werner Forman
Archive: 12bl, 13t, 22tl, 26bl, 27. Dennis Gargarin/istockphoto: 4tl.
Hanne Melbye-Hansen /istockphoto: 5. Goran Heckler/Alamy:
8b. Rolf Hicher/Alamy: 7. Historiska Museet
Stockholm/Bridgeman Art Library: front cover b. London Art
Archive/Alamy: 22br. Picturepoint/Topfoto: 4br. Lore Elisa
Ploughmann /istockphoto: 14bl. Prehistoric Museum Moesgard
Højberg /Gianni Dagli Orti/Art Archive: 15b. Private Collection
/Heini Schneebeli/Bridgeman Art Library: 11. Reuters /Corbis:
18bl. Henrik Sendelbach: 13bl. Ted Spiegel/Corbis: 14tr. Paul
Tessier/istockphoto: 15t. Ullsteinbild/Topfoto: 23. Manuel Velasco
/istockphoto: 21. Viking Ship Museum Oslo/Bridgeman Art
Library: front cover tr. Frederick Wall/istockphoto: 8t. York
Archaeological Trust: front cover tl, 1, 6bl, 9, 10bl, 10cr, 16bl, 16tr,
17, 19, 20tr, 24bl, 25. Felix Zaska/Corbis: 6tr. Every attempt has
been made to clear copyright. Should there be any inadvertent
omission please apply to the publisher for rectification.

March 2010
RD/6000006414/002

Note to parents and teachers: Every effort has been made by
the publishers to ensure that the web sites at the back of the
book are suitable for children, that they are of the highest
educational value, and that they contain no inappropriate
material. However, because of the nature of the Internet, it is
impossible to guarantee that the contents of these sites will
not be altered. We strongly advise that Internet access is
supervised by a responsible adult.

Contents

Many of the images in these book are imagined reconstructions of Viking scenes, supplied by Viking museums throughout Europe. They are based on the latest scientifically accurate archeological research. For more information, see page 7.

The Viking Age

The Vikings were Scandinavian people who lived in the countries we now call Norway, Sweden, and Denmark. Between the eighth and the eleventh century, the Vikings raided, explored, and settled in new lands.

▲ The Vikings built their homes on the flatter land near the shore, just as people do in Norway today (above).

Viking Homelands

In Norway and northern Sweden, most of the land is mountainous, rocky, or covered with forests. The climate is harsh, with cold, long, dark winters. It was hard for the Vikings to farm in these tough lands. In Denmark and southern Sweden, the land is flatter and easier to farm.

Raiders

The Vikings had a fierce reputation as warriors and raiders. Their raiding began in A.D. 793 when they attacked a monastery on the island of Lindisfarne off the coast of northern England. The Vikings killed monks, stole anything of value, and took prisoners to sell as slaves. They continued raiding in Britain, France, Germany, Spain, and Italy until the middle of the ninth century.

▼ Raiding Vikings traveled in longships.

▼ The Vikings traveled long distances, exploring new lands and trading their goods.

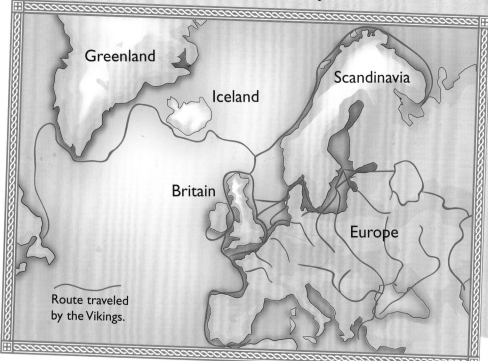

Route traveled by the Vikings.

Explorers and Settlers

The Vikings were skillful shipbuilders and sailors who traveled huge distances by sea and river. They explored and discovered new lands such as Iceland and Greenland, and were the first Europeans to land in North America, which they named Vinland. Some Viking families moved from their home countries to settle in new colonies such as Iceland, Greenland, France, Italy, and Britain.

The End of the Viking Age

The Viking age lasted for about 300 years. It came to an end as the Vikings adopted new ways of life. Those who settled in new lands started to follow the customs of local people. Vikings living in their homelands gradually changed from worshiping the Norse gods (see pages 26-27) and became Christians with a more peaceful way of life.

▲ Christian Vikings built magnificent wooden churches to worship in.

5

Family Life

Viking children grew up in a household with lots of people. They lived with their parents, brothers, sisters, grandparents, unmarried aunts, and sometimes servants and slaves. Children were cared for by female relatives.

Which Class?

Viking society was divided into three different classes. Jarls were rich, powerful noblemen who had lots of land and servants. Below them were the karls, or freemen, who were farmers, landowners, warriors, and traders. At the lowest level of Viking society were the thralls, or slaves, who were owned by rich Vikings. They had no rights and had to work hard. Thralls were often people who had been captured in raids.

▲ A reconstruction showing a Viking trader and his wife at work.

Worth Keeping?

When a Viking baby was born, it was shown to its father and he decided if it was worth keeping. Weak, sickly, or deformed babies were taken outside and left to die. If a baby was strong and healthy, the father sprinkled it with water and gave it a name before returning it to the mother.

◀ This reconstructed Viking scene shows a mother and father with two healthy children.

Viking Reconstructions

Modern reconstructions of Viking scenes are pieced together carefully using archeological evidence. At the Jorvik Viking Center in York, England, for example, everything you see is based on evidence unearthed between 1979-1981. Archeologists started digging on the site of an old candy factory, and unearthed remains of tenth-century Viking-age buildings. They also found an incredible 40,000 objects, ranging from clothing to a Viking toilet. These finds provided experts with a unique insight into Viking life in Britain.

Family Loyalty

Viking children were taught to be very loyal to all members of their family. Families supported their relations even if they had done something wrong. If one member of a family was hurt or insulted, it was everyone's duty to seek revenge.

▲ All the members of this Viking family would support each other in difficult times, as shown in this modern-day reconstruction.

Viking Homes

All Viking children lived in longhouses. These were rectangle-shaped, one-roomed houses where the family ate, worked, played, and slept. In winter, some Vikings also kept their animals in a cowshed at one end of the longhouse.

The Longhouse

Longhouses were made of wood in countries where there were plenty of trees, or from stone and turf in places such as Iceland. A fire for cooking and heating burned in a stone-ringed hearth in the center of the earthen floor. Smoke drifted out through a hole in either end of the roof.

◄ The roof of this reconstructed Viking house is thatched with dried straw.

Home Comforts

The homes that Viking children lived in were dimly lit because longhouses rarely had windows. Light came from the fire or oil lamps. Most families did not have much furniture. Raised platforms along the sides of the longhouse were used for both sitting on during the day and for sleeping on at night.

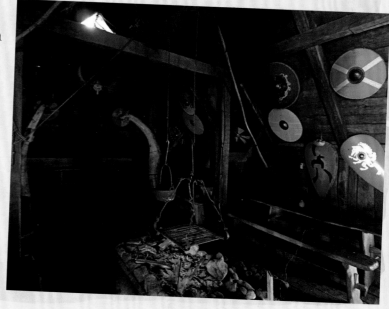

► The air inside longhouses was often smoky from the open fire.

No Bathroom

Viking longhouses did not have bathrooms. Children had to use an outside toilet that was often built around the back of the longhouse. It was a deep hole in the ground with a wooden seat on top. The toilet was surrounded by a screen made from wood. In winter it would have been very cold and in summer, very smelly. Instead of toilet paper, wool from a sheep would have been used.

▶ Viking toilets were situated outside the longhouse, as shown in this reconstruction.

Iceland Homes

In Iceland, archeological evidence shows that the Vikings made their longhouses from the building materials they found there. They used stones to make the foundations and made the walls and roof from turf. The walls were lined with wood paneling to keep out the cold and damp. These houses had good insulation and were warm in the winter and cool in the summer.

A Girl's Life

The Vikings did not have schools. Girls stayed at home and were taught how to run a home by their mothers and grandmothers. They would use these skills to look after their own home when they married.

Running a Home

Girls were taught how to prepare and cook food. They had to learn how to grind wheat into flour, bake bread, milk cows, churn butter, and make cheese. Clothes were made from scratch, so girls were taught how to spin wool from a sheep's fleece, weave it on a loom, and dye the cloth using vegetable dyes.

▲ Viking women and girls would have been busy working at home when the men were away, as shown in this reconstructed scene.

Being Independent

Viking men were often away from home either fighting, on raids, or trading. Women had to be independent and look after the family farm or business while the men were away. Girls were taught how to care for the farm and livestock so that they could manage when they married and their own husbands went away.

▲ This reconstruction shows a young girl spinning wool on a spindle, watched over by her mother.

Girl Warriors

Some girls were taught how to fight so they could defend their homes while the men were away. Freydis Eriksdottir, the daughter of the Viking king, Eric the Red, was taught how to become a warrior. She led an expedition to Vinland in North America. There are stories that tell how she fought Native Americans to protect her family and her possessions.

Getting Married

Girls were allowed to get married when they became adults at 12 years old. A girl's husband was chosen for her by her father, and usually she had no say in who she married. A dowry was paid to her new husband's family and a bridal price was paid back to her family from them. The bridal price depended on how much it was thought the girl was worth.

▼ A Viking bride and groom gave each other wedding rings like this one.

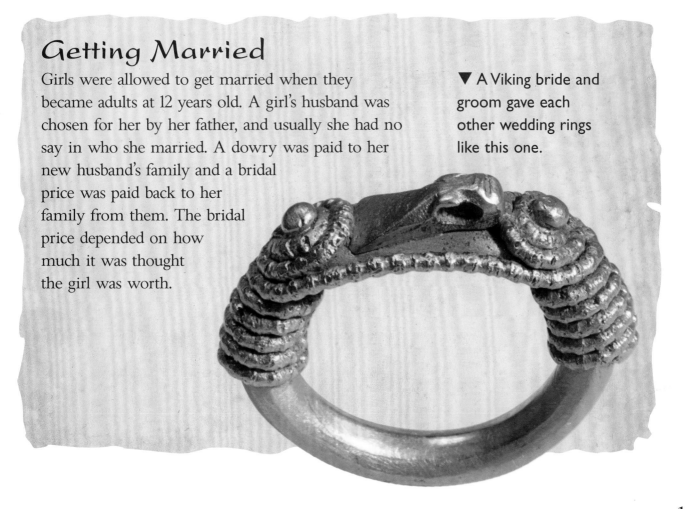

11

Viking Boys

Viking boys had to learn the skills they would need to survive when they became adults at the age of 12. They were taught all they needed to know by the adults they lived and worked with.

New Home

When boys reached the age of five, they were often sent away from home to live with another family. This was usually the family of an uncle or other respected and trusted member of the community. Boys learned all the skills they would need as an adult at their new home. This tradition strengthened the bonds between families.

▶ This boy is learning the skills needed to make a longship.

Warrior Training

Boys had to learn to fight so that they could be warriors and follow their king into battle or take part in a raid. They were trained how to use Viking weapons, such as the sword, axe, spear, bow, and arrow, as well as how to protect themselves with a shield.

◀ This Viking carving shows boys training to fight.

Learning a Trade

Most Vikings were farmers, so many boys learned the skills needed to run a farm, such as growing crops and looking after animals. Some boys were taught trades such as shipbuilding, blacksmithing, or shoemaking. A few boys would have been taught to read and write and may have become rune masters (see below).

▶ This Norwegian church carving shows a boy learning to make tools and weapons at a blacksmith's forge.

Writing Runes

The Vikings wrote in letters called runes (see pages 28-29). There were 23 runes and some stood for more than one sound. The runes were written with straight lines so that they could be carved into wood, bone, or stone. Runes were used to write the owner's name on things such as swords, on memorial stones, and for writing magic charms.

Meal Times

Viking families produced most of their own food. They grew crops and kept animals for meat and milk. They also fished and hunted wild animals. Children helped with growing and finding foods, and girls helped with cooking.

On the Menu

Children ate two meals a day, one in the morning and the other in the early evening. They ate from wooden bowls or platters, and used their fingers and sometimes a small spoon to pick up their food. Meals included red meat, fish, chicken, meat broths and stews, eggs, cheese, bread, porridge, apples, wild berries, and nuts, and vegetables such as cabbages, onions, and peas. They drank buttermilk, water, or ale.

▼ Meals were often cooked in a cauldron that hung over the fire.

▲ The Vikings gathered or hunted all these foods from the wild.

Hunting and Gathering

Vikings hunted for wild meat from animals such as deer, seals, rabbits, foxes, bears, whales, and seabirds. They caught fish from the sea or rivers. Children helped to collect shellfish, seabirds' eggs, and hazelnuts, and berries and fruits, such as wild raspberries, strawberries, plums, and cherries.

Puffin Hunting

In Iceland, people still hunt puffins and collect wild birds' eggs just as their Viking ancestors did. They catch flying puffins with large nets on the end of a pole. Puffin hunting is dangerous because the hunters have to balance carefully on the edge of tall cliffs. The puffins they catch are often eaten roasted.

Storing for Winter

Foods that were plentiful in the summer months were preserved and stored in jars or barrels for the long winter months. Viking girls had to learn how to preserve food as part of running the home. They were taught how to preserve fish and meat by pickling it in salt water or by hanging it out on racks in the wind to dry.

▶ A Viking jar like this was used to store food in the winter months.

15

What to Wear

Viking children dressed in smaller versions of the clothes their parents wore. Their clothes were hard-wearing and warm, to suit the cold weather in Viking lands.

Children's Clothes

Boys wore pants with a long-sleeved shirt like a tunic on top. Girls wore an ankle-length, long-sleeved dress called a chemise, with a shorter, open-sided overdress on top, which was fastened at the shoulders with brooches. All children wore underwear underneath their outer clothes to help them keep warm. In cold weather, they wore cloaks or shawls.

▼ The children in this reconstructed scene are dressed in traditional Viking clothing, and are playing hnefatafl (see pages 22–23).

▲ These leather Viking shoes were found at Jorvik (see page 19).

From Head to Toe

Viking children wore leather shoes or boots made from goatskin or calfskin, which were sometimes fastened with a leather thong or a toggle. Boys' hair was shoulder length. Girls grew their hair long and wore it in braids or loose. In cold weather, boys wore wool hats and girls wore scarves.

Homemade

Children's clothes were usually made at home by their mothers. They were made from wool or linen cloth, which was often dyed either brown, red, yellow, or blue using vegetable dyes. Sometimes children's clothes had decorative borders and embroidery around the neck of tunics or dresses.

▼ These are the remains of some Viking clothes that were discovered by archeologists at Jorvik (see page 19).

SIFTING THE EVIDENCE

On a Viking's Feet

We know what Vikings wore inside their shoes because archeologists have found a knitted sock at Jorvik (see page 19). Finding Viking clothes is rare because fabric and cloth rot easily. The sock survived because the waterlogged soil that it was buried in protected it from decaying. The sock was made using a technique called naalbinding (needle binding), which uses one needle and a piece of wool.

New Lands

Some Viking children left their homelands and moved to a new country. They traveled in Viking ships with their family and all their possessions, including the animals they owned. They often traveled long distances across open sea.

Setting Sail

Viking ships were fast, strong boats, but life on board was not very comfortable. There were no cabins on a Viking boat, so on voyages to new lands, children would often have been cold and wet. They had to sleep outside in oilskin sleeping bags and wrapped in animal fur to keep warm. Their meals were cold, dried fish and meat, hard bread, and fruit.

▶ Viking longships were built for speed, not for comfort, as this nineteenth-century illustration shows.

New Homes

Some Viking children moved to countries such as England or France, where there were already towns and settlements with people living in them. Other families settled in much harsher lands, such as Iceland and Greenland, where the weather was much colder and farming was difficult.

◀ A Viking man and his wife outside their home in an Icelandic reconstruction.

Viking Words

Many of the words we use today come from the Vikings. The days of the week are named after Viking gods. Tuesday is from Ty's day, Wednesday comes from Wodin's day, Thursday comes from Thor's day, and Friday is from Frigga's day. Other words such as anger, happy, call, take, sky, fellow, law, leg, egg, freckle, window, and knife are all Viking words.

Place names in Europe with these endings show where Vikings settled and lived.

toft—farm

thwaite—clearing

holm—small island or mound

carr—marsh

gate—road

by—farm

beck—stream

tarn—small lake

wick—harbor

Jorvik

Jorvik was home to many Viking children. It was the biggest Viking town in England, with a population of around 10,000 people. It was a thriving place with many Viking craftsmen, such as shoemakers, metalworkers, and carvers. The modern town of York is built on Jorvik.

▶ This reconstructed Viking street is in the Jorvik Center in York, in England.

Health and Hygiene

Children in Viking families had more baths than the Anglo-Saxons in Britain. They took a bath once a week on a Saturday and even named the day after the Viking word for bath.

Viking Medicine

When children got sick, they were taken to a doctor because the Vikings did not have them. Instead, their mother would give them some medicine made from herbs. The Vikings also tried curing sicknesses by using spells and carving runes onto pieces of bone, which they put under a sick person's pillow.

▼ Herbs such as angelica were used to treat many illnesses.

▲ Vikings used combs such as this one (shown above with its case) to remove head lice from their hair.

Viking Combs

Archeologists have found many combs that were used by Vikings to take care of their long hair. Combing helped to keep their hair tidy and also removed head lice and fleas. The combs that have been found were made from antlers or animal bones. Sometimes they were kept in a case to protect the delicate teeth of the comb.

Steam Bath

Viking children had their weekly bath in a small building called a bathhouse. Inside the bathhouse, stones were heated on a fire until they were red hot. Throwing water onto the stones filled the room with steam. People sat in the steamy room and, as they sweated, the dirt was washed off their skin. Afterward, they sometimes went outside and rolled in the snow to freshen up.

◄ These stones were used in a Viking bathhouse.

Unwanted Guests

Viking children had different parasites living on or in their bodies. They had headlice, fleas, and body lice on the outside. The remains from a Viking toilet in Jorvik show that the Vikings had whip worms and maw worms living inside them in their intestines. These worms could have made children feel sick.

Toys and Games

Viking children did not have as many toys as children do today. The toys they did have were usually made at home from wood. Some children also kept pets, such as dogs, cats, ferrets, and hawks, which they used to hunt with.

▲ These Viking king and soldier pieces were used to play hnefatafl.

Board games

Board games were popular with Viking children and adults. A game called hnefatafl (say neff-tah-fell), meaning kings table, was a battle game involving a king and his soldiers surrounded by an enemy army. One player had the king and eight other pieces. The other player had 16 pieces and his aim was to surround the king. The king started at the center and had to find his way through the enemy, to the side of the board.

Wooden Toys

Children had carved wooden toys that were miniature versions of the real things used by adults. They played with wooden swords, spears, and longships. They also had wooden animals and dolls. Archeologists have found Viking wooden toys during excavations.

▼ A replica of a toy Viking longship.

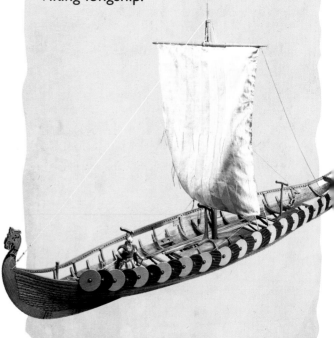

Lewis Chessmen

The Vikings who traveled to the East saw Arabs playing chess. They brought the game back with them, and were some of the first Europeans to play the game that we still play today. A complete set of Viking chessmen was found on the Isle of Lewis in the Hebrides Islands off of Scotland. The pieces are carved from walrus tusks and were probably lost on the way to being sold in England.

Outdoor Games

Viking children enjoyed playing outside. They played running and chasing games, a kind of soccer, and fought each other in pretend battles.

In cold weather, they played a bat-and-ball game called kingy bats. In summer, they swam, rowed in boats, and had competitions to see who could throw a heavy boulder the farthest.

▼ These children are enjoying a Viking game that tested their throwing skills.

Having Fun

Viking children had to work hard, but they also enjoyed having fun at feasts and celebrations. Huge feasts that lasted for days were held to celebrate seasonal events, such as Yule at midwinter, a marriage, or the successful return of a raiding party.

Feast Time

Everyone dressed in their best clothes for a feast. At the feast there was plenty of food and drinks. After the meal, children and adults enjoyed playing games, listening to poets, storytellers, and musicians, and watching dancers, jugglers, and acrobats perform.

▶ A nineteenth-century illustration shows a Viking feast, with a musician playing a small harp.

Sweet Music

Some children learned to play musical instruments. The Vikings played flutes made from the leg bones of cows, deer, or large birds, recorders made from bones or cow horns, wooden panpipes, lyres, harps, and drums.

◀ These Viking musical instruments were found in excavations at Jorvik.

Winter Sports

During the winter months, Viking children had fun sledding, skiing, and ice-skating. They wore ice skates made from the leg bones of horses tied onto boots or shoes with a strip of leather threaded through a hole in the bone. They skated by pushing themselves along with a pointed iron stick like a ski pole.

▼ Vikings called their ice skates, like this one, ice legs.

Shetland Festival

Each year on the last Tuesday of January, people in Shetland, a group of islands at the very top of Britain, celebrate their Viking past at the Up Helly Aa festival. In the town of Lerwick, men dress as Vikings and parade through the streets in a torch-lit procession. Then they set a replica longship on fire and sing Viking songs before going to parties that last all through the night.

Stories and Gods

During the Viking age, children were taught to believe in many different gods and goddesses. They thought the gods all lived together, in a place called Asgard, in a big family.

Worshiping the gods

The Vikings believed that each god and goddess controlled a different part of human life. Law and order were controlled by the god Thor, and love and beauty were the responsibility of the goddess Freya. The Vikings kept the gods happy by praying to them and giving them presents such as a sacrificed chicken or sheep.

▶ The god Thor carried a hammer. Vikings carried a charm of Thor's hammer like this one, to bring them luck.

▲ An illustration from a Viking story.

Story Time

During the long, dark winter nights, the Vikings sat around their fires telling stories. Children heard stories about the adventures of gods, heroes, and great battles. They learned the stories by heart so that they would be able to tell them to their own children when they grew up.

Sigurd the Dragon Slayer

One of the legends that children were told was the tale of Sigurd the dragon slayer. Sigurd became famous and rich by slaying the dragon Fafnor with his sword. The story involves magic, betrayal, and the hero being saved when he learns to understand the language of birds.

▶ This carved doorway from a church in Hylestad, Norway, shows the adventures of Sigurd.

Viking Sagas

The Vikings did not write down their stories. They were passed down from generation to generation by word of mouth. The stories were first written down in the twelfth and thirteenth centuries, after the Viking age had ended. These great tales are called sagas and we can still find out about the adventures of the Viking gods and heroes by reading them today.

Activities

Why not try some of the activities below to experience what Viking life might have been like for a child?

Write Like a Viking

Why not try writing your name in Viking runes? Use the key to work out which runes you'll need for your name. You could also use runes to write a secret Viking message to your friends.

Cook Like a Viking

Make some Viking oatcakes. These are simple to make and are delicious with cheese or your favorite topping. Ask an adult to help you with this task.

Ingredients:

- 3 cups whole-wheat flour
- 1 3/4 heaping cups oatmeal
- a pinch of salt
- 2 tablespoons vegetable oil
- cold water to mix

Method:

1. Mix the flour, oatmeal, salt, and vegetable oil together in a large bowl, then slowly add enough cold water, mixing all the time, until you have a fairly wet dough. Cover with a damp cloth and leave for 30 minutes.

3. Flour your hands, take a small handful of dough (about the size of a table tennis ball), and shape it into a round ball and then flatten into an oatcake shape.

4. Cook each oatcake on a hot skillet for about 30 seconds on each side. Eat the oat cakes hot or cold.

Read some Viking Myths and Sagas

Read some stories about the myths, sagas, gods, and monsters that Viking children listened to around the fire on cold winter nights.

The Saga of Erik the Viking by Terry Jones.

Viking!: Myths of Gods and Monsters by Kevin Crossley Holland.

The Vikings (Stories from Ancient Civilization) by Shahrukh Husain.

Dress Like a Viking

Make a simple Viking outfit from everyday clothes.

Boys: Make a tunic from a man's long-sleeved old shirt. Either cut off the collar or tuck it down inside and wear a belt around the waist. Wear loose pants and leather shoes or boots.

Girls: Wear a long-sleeved, ankle-length dress. An overdress can be made from an old sheet cut into two rectangles that reach from your shoulder to knees, and pinned together at the shoulders with safety pins. Wear leather shoes or boots on your feet.

An old curtain can be used for a cloak.

Play a Riddle Game

Vikings loved making up riddles like this one to entertain each other.

A marvel with eight feet,
four eyes, and knees
higher than its body.

What am I?
A spider

I need to be fed
But I have no mouth
If you care for me well
I will keep you warm
And give you light.

What am I?
A fire

Make up your own riddles and try them out on your friends. Can they guess the answers?

Timeline

A.D. 793 First attack on England at a monastery on Lindisfarne island off the coast of Northumberland.

795 First Viking raids on Ireland.

799 First Viking raids on France.

800 Vikings land in Orkney, Shetland, and the Faroe Islands.

810 Vikings raid present-day Netherlands and northern Germany.

836 Vikings settle and form the new town of Dublin in Ireland.

860 Vikings trade in Russia. Vikings attack Constantinople in Turkey.

866 Large Viking force lands in England looking for land to settle on.

867 Vikings capture York and rebuild it as Jorvik.

870 Discovery of Iceland.

874 Vikings start to settle in Iceland.

911 Vikings start to settle in France in an area we now call Normandy.

954 Erik Bloodaxe becomes the last Viking ruler of Jorvik.

960 King Harald Bluetooth of Denmark converts the country to Christianity.

980 Eric the Red is forced to leave Iceland.

982 Eric the Red discovers Greenland.

986 Vikings first sight the coast of North America.

995 King Olaf of Norway makes his people convert to Christianity.

1001 Leif the Lucky (son of Erik the Red) becomes the first European to land in North America. Founds a short-lived colony called Vinland.

1066 The Normans, descendants of Norwegian Vikings who settled in Normandy in northern France, invade England. The English king, Harold, is killed at the battle of Hastings. The leader of the Normans, William the Conqueror, becomes king of England.

1100 End of the Viking age. Viking settlers become part of local populations.

Glossary and Further information

antlers horns of a deer.

archeologist person who studies the past by digging up bones and objects.

climate general weather conditions of an area.

dowry money or property given by a woman's family to the husband.

hawk small falcon bird of prey.

intestines tubes inside the body that food passes through as it is digested.

longship type of boat the Vikings made.

lyre stringed musical instrument like a small harp.

monastery place where monks live.

monks men who devote their lives to God and live together in a religious group.

parasite plant or animal that lives on another living thing and gets all its food from it.

preserve to treat food by salting or drying it so that it does not go rotten.

replica copy of something.

rune a letter, or character, belonging to the written language of the Vikings.

sacrifice kill an animal or person as a gift to please the gods.

trader person who buys and sells goods.

vegetable dyes plants such as lichen, nettles, onions, beets, and berries that are used to color cloth.

waterlogged soil soil that contains a lot of water and is very wet.

Finding Out More about Life for Viking children

There are museums and web sites you can visit to find out more about Viking children.

www.vikinganswerlady.com
This site has lots of information about Viking life. Listen to how Viking instruments would have sounded, find out about the games they played, and discover what names the Vikings gave their children.

http://www.viking.no/
The Viking Network is an extensive web site all about the Vikings, and includes a quiz.

www.pbs.org/wgbh/nova/vikings/village.html
Use this website to take a "virtual walk" around a Viking village.

http://www.mnh.si.edu/vikings/start.html
Sail the stormy seas of the North Atlantic in your own Viking longboat with the help of this Smithsonian Institution web site.

www.jorvik-viking-centre.co.uk
The Jorvik Center in York, in England, has reconstructed Viking streets based on the evidence found in excavations.

Index